j383.14
GREENE, CAROL

Postal workers deliver our mail
$14.95

3.99

APR   2004

POSTAL WORKERS
DELIVER OUR MAIL

Design and Art Direction
Lindaanne Donohoe Design

Library of Congress Cataloging-in-Publication Data

Greene, Carol.

Postal workers deliver our mail/by Carol Greene.

p.   cm.

Summary: Describes the jobs done by the many workers
who contribute to the delivery of our mail.

ISBN 1-56766-403-2 (lib. bdg.)

1. Postal service — United States — Employees — Juvenile literature.
[1. Postal service.] I. Title.

HE6499.G74   1997   97-4239
383'.14'02373—dc21   CIP
                                        AC

POSTAL WORKERS
DELIVER OUR MAIL

By Carol Greene
Photographs by Phil Martin

THE CHILD'S WORLD®

VROOM! PLOP! CLICK! THUMP!
Many kinds of postal workers take care
of the mail. They do many different
kinds of jobs.

This postal worker picks up the mail

from mailboxes. *PLOP! PLOP!*

She takes it to the post office.

PLOP!

Some postal workers drive trucks.

VROOM! VROOM!

They pick up the mail from post offices.

Then they take it to a big postal center.

Workers at the postal center

work at machines.

This machine sorts the mail.

CLACK! CLACK!

Big packages go to one place.

KAPLUNK!

Letters go to another.

This machine puts a postmark over

the stamp on each envelope.

THUMP! THUMP!

The postmark shows where and when

the envelope was mailed.

Now no one can use the stamp again.

This machine reads the ZIP code.

HUMMMM! It prints a bar code.

BZZZZZ!

These numbers and marks tell another machine where the mail is going.

This machine reads the bar code.

CLICK! CLICK!

It puts all the mail for each area

in a special bin.

Some postal workers make sure all the machines work together smoothly. *HUMMM!*

VROOM!

Every day trucks go to the airport.

They take mail that is going far away.

Other trucks pick up mail that
has come from far away.
That mail goes to the postal center.
There, workers sort the mail.
Then trucks deliver the mail to the
different post offices.

Letter carriers get to the post office early.

First, the letter carriers put their mail

in order by checking the addresses.

Then each one takes mail to different

streets.

Letter carriers deliver the mail.

Some drive a little truck.

PUTT!   PUTT!

Other letter carriers walk.

They carry the mail in a big mailbag.

Some use mail carts.

Letter carriers work outdoors

in all kinds of weather.

And, thanks to all these postal workers—

Rebecca gets a birthday card from her grandma!

Questions and Answers

What do postal workers do?
Postal workers do all sorts of jobs. Some run machines. Some sell stamps. Others drive trucks. Most deliver the mail to homes and businesses.

How do people learn to be postal workers?
Most postal workers learn their jobs from other postal workers. Some go only to high school. Others go to college too. All postal workers work for the United States government.

What kind of people are postal workers?
Many kinds of people are postal workers. Some like to work with machines. Others like to work outdoors. And some like to drive trucks. But all postal workers must want to do a good job. They have an important task. They must get the mail through—no matter what!

How much money do postal workers make?
Postal workers make about $24,000 a year. After ten years of work they make about $30,000 a year.

GLOSSARY

address—the name, number and street, city and state, and zip code of the person to whom mail is sent

airport—the place where airplanes take off and land

bar code—special arrangement of lines, or bars, that have meaning and can be used to identify something

bin—a container; box

deliver—to hand over

letter carriers—a name for people who deliver mail

mail—letters, magazines, packages, and other objects delivered by postal workers

mailboxes—special places built to hold mail until it is picked up by postal workers

postal center—building that receives mail from smaller post offices

postmark—special mark showing date and place that is put over the stamp on every piece of mail

post offices—places where postal workers accept and sort mail for delivery and where people can buy stamps

stamp—a printed piece of paper sold by the government that must be on mail before it can be delivered by postal workers

zip code—special series of numbers used to identify mail addresses. For example, the first three numbers identify a certain place (often a city), the next set of numbers tell the postal workers in what part of the city the mail is to be delivered.

CAROL GREENE has written over 200 books for children. She also likes to read books, make teddy bears, work in her garden, and sing. Ms. Greene lives in Webster Groves, Missouri.